HOW THE WOLF BECAME THE DOG

HOW THE WOLF BECAME THE DOG

John Zeaman

Before They Were Pets

FRANKLIN WATTS
A Division of Grolier Publishing
New York London Hong Kong Sydney
Danbury, Connecticut

Cover and interior design by Robin Hoffmann
Illustration p. 18 by Karen Kuchar
Illustrations pp. 11, 22, 28, 33, 35, 39, 64 by Stephen Savage

Photographs ©: Animals Animals: 14 (Ken Cole), 35 (Gerard Lacz), 32 top right (Ralph R. Reinhard), 17 (Anup Shah), 33 (Fred Whitehead); AP/ Wide World Photos: 49; Art Resource: 20; Comstock: 51 (Townsend P. Dickenson), 6, 39, 41, 44, 52; Folio, Inc.: 26 (Everett C. Johnson); Gamma-Liaison: 47 (Spencer Grant), 46 (Sam Sargent); National Geographic Society: 19 (Richard T. Nowitz); Photo Researchers: 24 top left (Frederic /Jacana), 2, 27, 32 bottom left (Tim Davis), 40 (Richard Hutchins), 21 (J.L Klein & M.L. Hubert/OKAPIA), 38 (William H. Mullins), 34 (Kees van den Berg), 24 top right (Jeanne White); PhotoEdit: 45 (Mary Kate Denny), 53 (Michael Newman); Superstock, Inc.: 31 (British Musuem, London); Tony Stone Images: 10 (Art Wolfe); Visuals Unlimited: 37 (John D. Cunningham), 13 (Joe McDonald).

> Visit Franklin Watts on the Internet at:
> http://publishing.grolier.com

Library of Congress Cataloging-in-Publication Data

Zeaman, John.
How the wolf became the dog / John Zeaman
p. cm. — (Before they were pets)
Includes bibliographical references (p.   ) and index.
Summary: Provides an overview of how wolves evolved into "man's best friends."
ISBN 0-531-11459-7 (lib. bdg.)   0-531-15906-X (pbk.)
1. Dogs—Juvenile literature. 2. Wolves—Juvenile literature. 3. Dogs—Behavior—Juvenile literature. 4. Wolves—Behavior—Juvenile literature. [1. Dogs. 2. Wolves.] I. Title. II. Series: Zeaman, John. Before they were pets.
SF426.5.Z43 1998
599.773—dc21   97-8321
                                                                                              CIP
                                                                                              AC

© 1998 by John Zeaman
All rights reserved. Published simultaneously in Canada
Printed in the United States of America
2 3 4 5 6 7 8 9 10 R 07 06 05 04 03 02 01 00 99

	Introduction 7
Chapter 1	The First Tamed Wolves 9
Chapter 2	Physical Changes 16
Chapter 3	Domestication 23
Chapter 4	Human-made Animals 30
Chapter 5	Why Is the Dog Man's Best Friend? 43
	Glossary 55
	For Further Information 57
	Index 61

All dogs are direct descendants of wild wolves.

INTRODUCTION

Humankind's first pet was an animal that we don't usually think of as particularly friendly, one that has a rather fearsome, though undeserved, reputation in fairy tales and adventure stories: the wolf.

In fact, the animal we now refer to as our best friend is that very same wolf. We may find this hard to believe at first, not only because wolves are wild, unfriendly animals but also because most dogs look so different from wolves. There is certainly a resemblance to wolves in such dogs as German shepherds or Siberian huskies, but other dogs—tiny Chihuahuas, elongated dachshunds, elegant poodles, spotted dalmatians—look nothing at all like wolves, or even much like each other. But scientists today agree that all dogs, regardless of their appearance, are direct descendants of wild wolves tamed by people. In fact, dogs still belong to the same **genus** as the wolf. Scientists call this genus *Canis*. Wolves are classified as *Canis lupus*, dogs as *Canis familiaris*. Because they belong to the same genus, a wolf and a dog can mate and have offspring together. A dog and a fox could not do this, nor could a wolf and a hyena. So, it's not at all wrong to say that a dog is really a type of wolf, although one that has been altered by thousands of years of breeding.

But how did people first make friends with wolves and gradually change them into the animal that we know today as the dog? Just how did this relationship get started?

CHAPTER 1: THE FIRST TAMED WOLVES

The process of taming wild animals and breeding them to produce new forms is called **domestication**. The domestication of wolves probably occurred about 25,000 years ago, but there is no recorded history of it. That's why this period and everything before it is known as prehistoric time. Early humans lived in hunter-gatherer societies and dwelled in caves or primitive shelters. They inhabited much of the world—Asia, Europe, Africa and North America. Wolves lived in many of these places, too. They lived in social groups very much like the people did and were probably drawn to human settlements by scraps and

Not So Ferocious

Wolves are shy animals. There has never been a documented case in North America of a wolf attacking a person.

A pack of gray wolves roams through a forest in Canada. Scientists estimate that humans began taming wolves about 25,000 years ago.

bones that humans threw away. But the wolves also hunted their own food. They hunted in packs, with organized strategies that allowed them to bring down animals much bigger than themselves. It is very likely that people observed these behaviors and learned from them. People may have used these techniques to hunt wolves!

About 18,000 years ago, during a period known as the Ice Age, great glaciers covered much of the Earth. In order to survive in the cold, people learned to make clothing from the furs of animals that they hunted. The best furs came from animals that had bushy winter coats, such as the arctic fox and the wolf. It is very likely that at some point people hunting wolves took home a wolf cub. Perhaps the mother was killed by the hunters, who brought the tiny, helpless cubs back to their settlement. Perhaps they wanted to eat the cubs or give them as playthings to young children. We know that contemporary tribal people enjoy taming young wild animals. For example, the Inuit—the native peoples of northern Canada, Alaska, Greenland, and eastern Siberia—tame wolves and breed them with their sled dogs to produce tougher, more hardy animals. Some Inuits even use tamed wolves in their dog teams.

When people first tamed wolves, a very strange and unexpected thing happened. Because wolves are instinctively social animals, they adapted quite readily to human communities. A young wolf cub bonded and identified with the people who raised it and saw itself as part of the human "pack." It developed a strong affection and attachment to its immediate family. As it matured, the wolf began to show its value to its early human masters.

Call of the Wild

The gray wolf has a very distinctive howl that can be heard from up to 10 miles (16 km) away. Howling is a form of communication used to reunite the pack, to greet other wolves, or for pure enjoyment.

HOW WOLVES COOPERATE

The wolf is a very social animal and depends on pack cooperation for its survival. Each pack is led by alpha wolves, a male and female, who are the only ones that breed. Below them are the two beta wolves, who are leaders of all the other wolves. At the very bottom of the pack are the pups.

The alpha wolves may lead the hunt, break trail in snow, or eat before the others do, but they don't always insist on this. They are not bullies. Wolves can't risk all-out fights with each other, because such fights could cause injuries or death, and this would hurt the pack as a whole.

Instead of fighting, wolves use body language and other displays to communicate and resolve disputes. An alpha wolf may hold another wolf's muzzle in its mouth to show that it is boss, or a submissive wolf may put its tail between its legs to show that it is not challenging the leader.

This ability to cooperate and accept leadership is what makes the descendants of wolves—dogs—such good pets.

Imagine the surprise of these people when they saw the wolf protecting them, guarding their camp from other predators or members of enemy tribes! In addition to guarding, wolves would have readily learned to help on the hunt. Together, human and wolf became a formidable hunting team, with wolves tracking and possibly treeing animals, and humans killing the prey with spears or arrows.

Two gray wolves hunt along a river. Cooperation is important for the survival of the wolf pack.

It probably wasn't long before every member of a community wanted such a helper.

As people tamed and bred more and more wolves, the wolves began to change. The changes were very slight at first. The wolves who were the tamest, the most loyal, and the best guards were kept and valued. If a wolf was too vicious or wild, then it was probably killed. As a result, a

Two young Inuits pose with their sled dog in Bathhurst Inlet, Canada. Today, the Inuit continue their tradition of taming wolves and breeding them with their sled dogs.

new **breed** of wolf gradually evolved—the ancestor of today's dog.

By about 15,000 years ago, wolves had become dogs, and people had likely established the close emotional relationship with them that we have today. One clue from the past shows the power of this bond: a 12,000-year-old grave in Israel containing a man buried with a puppy. The man's arm rests affectionately on the animal's shoulder.

CHAPTER 2: PHYSICAL CHANGES

How did the dog come to look so different from the wolf? First, it's important to understand that not all wolves look alike. Wolves come in a variety of sizes. The smallest—the Arabian desert, or Indian wolf—weighs only 45 pounds (20 kg), and the biggest, which lives in the arctic tundra, can weigh as much as 200 pounds (91 kg). Scientists don't believe that these large arctic wolves contributed very much to today's dog, however. Most of the wolf skeletons they have found in human settlements are of smaller wolves. One of the most frequently found skeletons is that of the smallish Asian wolf called *Canis lupus pallipes.*

In India, an Asian wolf chases its prey. Scientists believe that the Asian wolf is the most likely ancestor of the dog.

When animals are domesticated by people, they gradually change over several generations until they begin to look different from their wild counterparts. No one is sure why this happens, but scientists believe it is a result of the animal's physical and emotional dependence on people. Domesticated animals tend to become smaller and to have more body fat, shorter jaws, and smaller teeth.

EARLY DOGS

Scientists would like to know exactly when wolves began to turn into dogs, but there is no precise way to know this. The best they can do is search sites where prehistoric people once lived and study the bones of the animals that they find there. This kind of scientific research is called **archaeology**. Doing archaeological work is often like trying to solve a mystery. Suppose, for example, that you

DOG ANATOMY

All dogs, regardless of their breed, share a common anatomy. They may have elongated bodies, flat faces, short legs, or droopy jowls, but they have the same skeletal structure, the same internal organs, and the same external body parts.

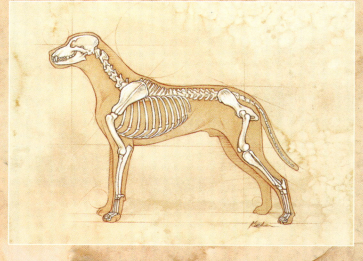

Archaeologists unearthed this dog skeleton at an excavation site in Israel. Scientists know that dogs definitely existed by 10,000 B.C.

were studying the remains of a 12,000-year-old settlement, and, among the bones of humans and the remains of their pots and weapons, you found some wolf bones. What would you conclude? Would you be right if you assumed that the bones were those of a pet wolf? They might be, but they could also be the bones of a wild wolf that had been hunted and killed for its skin or meat. Archaeologists can sometimes tell if an animal was eaten by the marks of tools left on the bones.

But if you found a lot of wolf skeletons, all intact and not in the same place, like food debris, you could probably assume that these were the bones of tame wolves who were part of the community. Then you might begin to study the wolf bones more carefully to see whether any of them were different in any way from those of wild wolves:

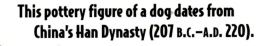

This pottery figure of a dog dates from China's Han Dynasty (207 B.C.–A.D. 220).

did they have smaller teeth, shorter jaws, and smaller bones?

The earliest record of dog remains comes from a cave in a place called Palegawra in what is now Iraq. The fossil isn't very much, really, just a part of the lower jaw called the mandible. This mandible, which is estimated to be 12,000 years old, is different than that of a wolf of the same period. It's smaller, and the teeth are more compact, especially the premolars. This is the very first evidence that wolves had begun to change into dogs, but scientists believe that domestication probably happened earlier.

Most of the bones of early dogs closely resemble those from the smaller species of wolves, which is why scientists say that dogs descended from these wolves, not from the larger ones. Larger bones, however, have been found at a place called Jarmo in northern Iraq. This settlement is much more recent than the one in Palegawra. It dates to 6600 B.C. (Remember, dates go backwards in B.C. time, so the larger numbers are from earlier times than the smaller numbers.) Once again, the archaeologists found only fragments, some from the skulls and some from the jawbones of the animals. The teeth are large, almost the same size as those of the large European wolf. But because they are not quite as big, scientists believe that these fragments represent a very early stage in the domestication of dogs, when they were still very close in appearance to wolves.

Why Do Dogs Pant?

A dog pants with its tongue out to cool itself. Evaporation of water from the mouth lowers the body temperature. Unlike people, dogs have efficient sweat glands only on their feet, so they can't cool off by sweating like we can.

THE MISSING LINK

Only recently have scientists concluded that dogs are descended directly from wolves. When archaeologists first studied the bones of early dogs, they thought they might be the bones of an ancient wild species of dog that was tamed by man, a missing link between today's dog and earlier canid ancestors.

Another theory was that dogs had two ancestors, the wolf and the jackal, and that some dog breeds were "jackal dogs" and others were "wolf dogs." Careful study showed that jackals are in fact very different from both wolves and dogs. But when scientists studied wolves, they found amazing similarities to dogs in almost all respects.

Wolves are like dogs in many respects. You can see the similarities between dogs and wolves in some dogs, such as this pair of Belgian sheepdogs.

America's Earliest Dogs

The earliest remains of dogs in the United States are fossils estimated to be 10,000 years old. They were unearthed at Jaguar Cave, an archaeological site in Idaho.

Another place where scientists have found remains that seem to be intermediate between dog and wolf is at Vlasac on the Danube River in Romania. Many of the 1,914 **canid** bones found there are definitely from small dogs, and some of these appear to have been eaten, because the bones had been chopped up. A few of the fragments, however, are between wolf and dog in size, and scientists believe that these belonged to wolves who had only been domesticated a few generations earlier and were just beginning to show the physical changes. The skeletal remains found in these early settlements are not all identical. Dogs had already begun to take on different forms. Some of them show what scientists call a **marked stop** in the shape of the skull—the place where the face slants sharply down right before the muzzle. Other dogs show the long, tapering muzzle of the greyhound.

It would be wrong, however, to say that dogs had already begun to divide into distinct breeds. There was nothing like the variety in size and shape that we find among modern-day dogs. For example, scientists recently compared three complete dog skeletons that were found in different parts of England: Windmill Hill, Easton Down, and Grime's Graves. All three date to a period around 2000 b.c. Each animal had a shoulder height of about 20 inches (51 cm), and their skulls had a similar shape.

It wasn't until later times that dogs began to vary so much. In the Roman period in England (A.D. 43–410), for example, dogs ranged in shoulder height from 9 inches (23 cm) to 28 inches (71 cm), as indicated from skeletal remains from that time.

CHAPTER 3
DOMESTICATION

We have discussed how wolves changed as a result of domestication and how they became smaller and gentler. But that doesn't explain how there came to be dogs in such an incredible variety of forms. To understand why dogs come in so many sizes, shapes, and temperaments, we need to understand the concept of breeding.

Man's relationship with the wolf began with taming, the process by which wild animals, usually young ones, are made less wild by gentle handling and feeding. In fact, the word "pet" is an agricultural term that originally came from this practice of raising animals by hand. The changes

Domestication has led to a variety of breeds. The Great Dane (right) is one of the largest dog breeds, and the Chihuahua (above) is one of the smallest.

How Well Do Dogs See?

Dogs see better in dim light than we do, and they pick up movement better, but they don't see all the detail we do. Their color vision is much weaker; bright colors probably appear as pale pastels to them.

that come about as a result of taming affect only each individual animal. The offspring of tame animals will not be born tame. Suppose you tamed a coyote and later that coyote had pups. The pups would have all the instincts and natural fears of a wild coyote, even though the mother was tame. If these young coyotes grew up around people and were handled and fed by them, they too would grow up tame. But this kind of tameness can't be inherited from parents. It is a learned behavior. Breeding, however, is different. Breeding is the only way that characteristics can be passed on from one generation of animal to another.

All living creatures inherit qualities from their parents. You have qualities that have been passed on to you from your mother and father. You may have your father's red hair and your mother's green eyes. If both your parents are tall, you are likely to be tall. This is because parents pass on **genes** to their children, and these genes carry coded instructions that determine many of our physical characteristics.

People do not marry and have children for the purpose of creating offspring who have green eyes and red hair. But people have been breeding animals for thousands of years to bring out qualities that are useful or attractive. Suppose, for example, that you wanted to produce a small breed of dog. How would you do it? First, you would need several mating pairs of dogs. Then, each time a litter was born, you would look for an unusually small puppy. Small pups like this are often called runts. You would then raise the runt to maturity and then try to mate it with a runt from another litter. The puppies born to these runts would tend to be small, and you would then select the smallest of these litters and breed them. By mating more and more generations of runts, you will produce dogs that will become consistently smaller. Eventually, over a period of years, you would create a new breed of small dog. This, in fact, is how the various toy, or miniature, breeds of dog were created. People wanted dogs small enough to fit in a lap, like a cat.

Selective Breeding

The process described above is known as **selective breeding**, and it can be used to develop any number of qualities, not just size. Dogs can—and have been—bred for color, coat type, ear shape, muzzle length, speed, sense of smell, and personality. It's hard to think of a dog trait that hasn't been modified by people through breeding.

In the beginning, prehistoric people probably didn't really understand what they were doing. The dogs were

Midget Dog

The smallest adult dog on record, according to the *Guinness Book of Pet Records*, was a freakish matchbox-size Yorkshire terrier that was only 2-1/2 inches (6.3 cm) at the shoulder and measured 3-3/4 inches (9.5 cm) from the tip of its nose to the base of its tail.

Generations of selective breeding resulted in the size and appearance of these two terriers.

changing as a result of people's preferences for certain qualities, but there wasn't intentional breeding. So how did this begin? Suppose, for example, that you were an early human and had a dog that produced a litter of puppies. Perhaps you decided to keep one of the puppies for yourself and let the others run wild. And, suppose that one of the puppies was very distinctive. Maybe it had a curled-up tail, was black and white instead of the normal wolf color, had large eyes, or had something else that made it different. You would probably want to keep that one because it was special and because everyone else in the community would recognize it as your dog.

FLOPPY EARS AND CURLED-UP TAILS

Dogs often differ from wolves in the characteristics of their tails, ears, and fur. Wolves have upright, triangular ears. But many dogs, such as poodles or golden retrievers, have floppy ears that hang straight down. In cocker spaniels, these ears are very elongated. Other dogs, such as the Pomeranian sheepdog or the greyhound, have ears whose tips flop forward, and the whippet's ears stick out sideways from its head.

Wolves have bushy, slightly curved tails. But dogs such as the Akita or the husky have tails that curl over and touch their backs, and the Italian greyhound's tail curls down between the back legs. Some dogs, like the Pembroke Welsh Corgi, have a short, stubby tail. (Many dogs that appear to have short tails actually have had them docked, or cut shorter, during puppyhood.)

Wolves also have bushy, straight-haired coats. But bulldogs have very short, nappy coats; poodles have curly coats; Airedale terriers have wiry coats; and the Yorkshire and Skye terriers have such long coats that they look like mops.

Despite being descended from the wolf, this Jack Russell terrier's physical features—including floppy ears and a short, nappy coat—are quite different from those of a wolf.

Barking Lessons

Wolves bark infrequently, and even then it is a quiet "woof" rather than a dog-type bark. However, a wolf kept with dogs will learn to bark.

This special one would grow up and breed with other dogs in the community, and it would pass on its unusual quality to at least some of its offspring. So, even though you didn't understand anything about breeding, your preference for a particular quality would end up producing more dogs having that quality. In a few years, a number of dogs in the community would have curled-up tails or black-and-white markings.

One quality that early people would have valued in a dog was a tendency to bark, because a barking dog makes a good guard. Today, we take it for granted that all dogs bark, but this was not a quality that came naturally to them from their wolf heritage. Barking is a behavior that is almost totally absent in wolves. Wolves and coyotes will bark occasionally in the wild, but the deep bark of the large breeds of dog, the baying of the bloodhound, and the yapping of the toy dogs is the result of domestication. Because early humans and their descendants found barking to be such a valuable quality in dogs and always kept the dogs that barked, more and more barking dogs would have been born and eventually this vocal tendency would have been bred into almost all dogs.

There is an even more unusual example of a quality that was bred into dogs, almost certainly by accident. Perhaps you have a seen a dog lift up the corners of its mouth in what looks very much like a smile. Many dogs show this tendency, especially if they live with a family in which there is a lot of affection between the family members and the dog. This, too, is a quality that is never found in wild wolves. It makes sense then that people probably bred this quality into dogs. Seeing a pet smile just like a human is obviously something that pleases people. Such dogs would have been preferred to other dogs and, once

28

again, would have had a greater opportunity to breed and have puppies. Some scientists believe that there is a learned aspect to this behavior and that dogs smile in imitation of their owners. There is probably some truth to this, but because wild wolves don't do it, it's likely that breeding is also responsible.

Eventually, people became more aware of the mechanism of inheritance. They realized that dogs and other animals could pass on specific traits and that people could mold dogs into the forms that would make them most useful. Intentional breeding had begun.

CHAPTER 4
HUMAN-MADE ANIMALS

Breeding is an incredibly powerful force. Think about how many different kinds of dogs there are and how dramatic the differences between them is. The St. Bernard, for example, is the heaviest breed of dog and can weigh more than 200 pounds (91 kg). The tallest dog, the Great Dane, can reach 42 inches (107 cm) at the shoulder. Contrast this with the smallest dog, the Chihuahua of Mexico. Some mature Chihuahuas weigh as little as 1.5 pounds (.7 kg) And one, whose skeleton is in the Museum of Natural History in Mexico City, measured only 7 inches (18 cm). Think of it: from 200 pounds (91 kg) to 1.5 pounds (.7 kg). From 7 inches

A dog appears in the lower righthand corner of the page in this Egyptian book.

(18 cm) high to 42 inches (107 cm) high—all in the same species.

We have discussed how dogs gradually changed and began to look very different from wolves. But when did the first distinct breeds arise, those dogs that we know of today as St. Bernards, dalmatians, poodles, or any of the other breeds? The first two breeds of dog were probably the greyhound and the mastiff. The carvings and murals of ancient Egypt show many different shapes and sizes of dogs. One that occurs frequently and was apparently a popular hunting dog that looks very much like the greyhound. With its long legs and thin, streamlined body, this dog was bred to be fast, which made it valuable for chasing down game. There is no way to know for sure whether this ancient hound is the same as the present-day greyhound, but it

An eight-month-old Italian greyhound shows its running technique. The greyhound looks very similar to a hunting dog popular with ancient Egyptians.

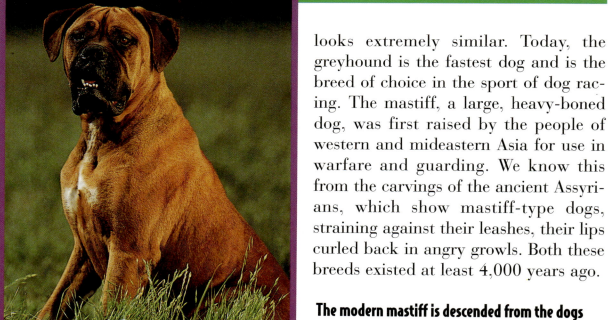

looks extremely similar. Today, the greyhound is the fastest dog and is the breed of choice in the sport of dog racing. The mastiff, a large, heavy-boned dog, was first raised by the people of western and mideastern Asia for use in warfare and guarding. We know this from the carvings of the ancient Assyrians, which show mastiff-type dogs, straining against their leashes, their lips curled back in angry growls. Both these breeds existed at least 4,000 years ago.

The modern mastiff is descended from the dogs raised by the peoples of western and mideastern Asia.

The Romans were probably the first Europeans to develop many distinct breeds of dogs. They raised dogs for speed, for retrieving, and even for warfare. They had large fighting dogs, similar to the mastiff, as well as tiny lap dogs. In the first century A.D., the Roman writer Pliny described these lap dogs, telling how "our dainty dames" make so much of "the pretty little dogs" and how they believed that such dogs could ease stomach pains if they were held close to the midsection. The Romans also had dogs for herding and guarding other domesticated animals, such as goats and sheep. Another Roman writer, Columella, an expert on agriculture, described in the first century A.D. just what type of dog was best for helping on a farm. Such a dog, he said, should be big and have a "loud and sonorous [boom-

A beagle barks at a stranger. Wanting good guard dogs, early humans valued dogs that barked.

33

A sheepdog stands watch over a herd of sheep in Italy. Many sheepdogs today are white because shepherds wanted a dog that wouldn't be mistaken for a wolf.

ing] bark," to scare away predators. If the dog was used to guard sheep, he said, it should preferably be white, so that it would not be mistaken for a wolf and be accidentally killed if the shepherds were driving off wolves in the dark. The present-day sheepdog, is, in fact, mostly white. The sheepdog's woolly appearance also makes it look something like a sheep, and people believe that this makes the dog less frightening to the sheep themselves, who might otherwise fear it as a wolf.

One of the most interesting chapters in the history of dog breeding concerns the Chinese Pekingese. The creation of this animal was an amazing feat of breeding and probably took thousands of years to accomplish. The Pekingese is not just small, it has a roundish face not unlike that of a human baby. It is this babyish quality that makes the dog so appealing to people. Think of how different the shape of that face is from that of the wolf. How could such a dog be bred from a wolf? The key to understanding the

A Pekingese has a round, babyish face. It took many generations of breeding to create the Pekingese.

How Well Do Dogs Hear?

For sounds of low pitch, a dog's ears have about the same ability as ours. But dogs can hear ultrasonic sounds that we can't, such as the high-pitched squealing of rodents or bats.

Pekingese is not in the mature wolf, but in the wolf before it is born, while it is still developing inside its mother. This is called the fetal stage. The Pekingese's flattened face, large brain case, big eyes, short legs, curly tail, and soft fur are all features of the unborn wolf. Occasionally puppies would have been born with these immature features. These dogs were probably used to breed the unusual Pekingese.

Over the centuries, dogs were bred by kings and aristocrats for sport, hunting, and companionship and became more and more specialized. The bloodhound, for example, was bred to have a very sensitive nose that could be used for tracking game. As a result, the breed has a sense of smell three million times more powerful than a human's. Bloodhounds have been credited with following trails of people or animals that are more than a week old. The dalmatian was bred with its fancy spots as a flashy coach dog that would run along next to the coach and horses. Later, firefighters adopted these dogs as mascots, and the dalmatians graduated from running beside the horse-drawn fire wagons to riding on the fire trucks. The greyhound was bred to have long legs and a slender body so that it could be used in high-speed chases, with men following on horseback. The basset hound, on the other hand, was bred to have shorter legs so that hunters on foot could keep up with it.

Terriers were bred to go into burrows after foxes, badgers, and rodents. For this reason they had to have unusually stubborn and feisty personalities so that they would keep after their prey when they were alone down in the burrow. The various retrieving dogs—such as Labradors, golden retrievers, and poodles—were bred to jump into

WOLF-DOG CROSSES

In recent years, some people have been breeding wolves and dogs together, creating a wolf-dog cross. The people who do this usually want a dog that will be tougher, or even scary to other people. Animal experts agree that this is usually not a good idea. By breeding wolves with dogs, people are undoing thousands of years of breeding that has made the dog a friendly, loyal, and reliable pet. Sometimes, these wolf-dogs cannot be housebroken. They are not protective of a house or a family, nor do they accept punishment as readily as a dog. Most important, wolf-dogs are often afraid of people, just as wild wolves are. As a result, there have been incidents of people being killed or badly bitten by wolf-dogs.

A wolf-dog hybrid is enclosed within a fence. Breeding wolves with dogs has become popular, but the behavior of these hybrids is often unpredictable.

water to retrieve game birds that had been shot by arrow or gun. For this job, they had to have a very cooperative, gentle temperament so they wouldn't crush the bird in their jaws or run off with it. This is why such dogs make good pets for children today.

The bulldog was developed as a savage fighter for bull-baiting contests. The dogs were expected to bite and hold onto bulls with their powerful jaws. Their short muzzle allowed them to breathe while they maintained their grip.

Champion Dog Owner

The greatest number of dogs owned by one person were the 5,000 mastiffs kept by the great Mongol emperor Kublai Khan (1215–94) for the purpose of fighting in arenas.

A Labrador retriever holds a pheasant in its mouth during a hunting trip in Idaho. Hunters bred retrievers to fetch game birds.

Oldest American Breed

The oldest American breed is the American foxhound, which dates back to 1650, when Englishman Robert Brooke settled in Maryland with his pack of foxhounds and crossed them with other strains of dog.

Humans bred bulldogs to fight bulls. They wanted a dog with a muscular body, short muzzle, and strong jaw.

Today, there are about 440 different breeds of dogs. Various organizations, such as the American Kennel Club (AKC), set standards for dog breeds and categorize them. For example, the AKC recognizes 130 breeds. Unfortunately, breeding has not always been beneficial to dogs, especially when people began to breed for unusual physical characteristics. Take the bulldog. Its short muzzle, which was so useful for fighting, also causes respiratory problems. Another exam-

Judges present a trophy to a winner at a dog show. Many people like showing off their dogs in dog shows.

ple is the Chinese shar-pei, a dog bred to have a very loose and wrinkly skin that some people find appealing. But, these dogs often have skin problems. Other dogs suffer from a predisposition to hip problems, blindness, deafness, or certain diseases.

FERAL DOGS

Dogs have been bred to be partners with people, and yet many dogs do not live with people. They have reverted to being wild, a condition known as being **feral**. In cities or other built-up places, feral dogs have a hard time surviv-

A dingo, a type of feral dog, stands in the wilds of Australia.

ing. But in some less-developed parts of the world, feral dogs live in packs, fending for themselves just like their wolf ancestors, although they often live more by scavenging than hunting. Some estimates say there are as many as 150 million feral dogs today. Some of these dogs are descended from dogs that returned to a wild existence many centuries ago. After a long period of breeding freely in the wild, without people's interference, these dogs take on a similar appearance. In Australia, this type of wild dog is known as a dingo. In New Guinea, it is the singing dog, in Asia the Piy dog, in the Middle East the pariah dog, and in the Americas the Indian dog.

CHAPTER 5: WHY IS THE DOG MAN'S BEST FRIEND?

Today, the dog enjoys a special closeness with man. But why is this? Why was the dog able to adapt so well to life with a different species? Why is the dog called "man's best friend?" The dog is intelligent, yes, but so are other animals, some more so than the dog. Why couldn't our best friend be the pig, the chimpanzee, or the elephant? Let's look at those qualities that have made the dog such a close friend of humans.

Dogs make great family pets and are often called "man's best friend."

HYGIENE

One very basic reason that the dog has become the human's best friend, one we take for granted, is **hygiene**. Because dogs can be housebroken, they are allowed the run of our houses. This makes them ideal companions. The ability of dogs to be housebroken comes from their

A girl walks her spaniel. For proper hygiene, dogs usually need to be walked twice a day.

Why Do Dogs Sniff the Ground So Much?

To get information about other dogs. By sniffing the urine and droppings left by other dogs, a dog can often tell if a dog was a male or a female, a puppy or a mature dog, even sometimes what mood the dog was in.

wolfish heritage. Wolves live in a fixed place or central den. Because of this, they developed the ability to deposit their urine and feces away from their home, a quality that they share with cats. Domesticated dogs bring this same tendency to the human house.

People who have pet dogs usually walk them twice a day. This happens to be the same twice-a-day routine that wolves have in the wild. One reason why monkeys or chimpanzees don't make good house pets is their hygiene habits. In the wild, they have no central home and eliminate wherever they please. So, even though chimpanzees are more intelligent than dogs, they are almost impossible to housebreak.

Dogs are friendly and make great companions. Just ask this boy and his dog.

A family relaxes at home with their dog. Dogs are social animals and become loyal to and protective of their human families.

Do Dogs Have a Sixth Sense?

Yes, dogs appear to have a sensitivity to changes in the Earth's magnetic field. This explains the ability of dogs to find their way home over long distances on unfamiliar terrain.

SIZE AND APPEARANCE

When it comes to size, the perfect pet is an animal that is big enough for us to relate to but not so big that it feels threatening. Very big animals are impractical as pets. We may love horses, but a horse cannot share our home and, in fact, needs a home of its own about the same size as ours.

At the same time, animals that are very small, like mice, are easy to keep in the house but can't be true companions. The size difference is too great. We can't really relate to a mouse face to face the way we can with a dog.

DOG HEROES

Dogs are so loyal to people that they will risk their own lives to protect or save them. Over the past 50 years there have been hundreds of newspaper accounts of dog heroism in the United States. Since 1954, the Ken-L Ration dog food company has presented an annual dog hero award. Of the 43 people saved by these dog heroes, 14 were from near-drowning, 5 from fires, 5 from animal attacks, and 3 from traffic accidents.

The most celebrated dog hero of all time was a St. Bernard named Barry, who, between the years 1800 and 1812, saved at least 40 people lost in blizzards or buried by avalanches in the Swiss Alps. Some stories say Barry was killed by the last person he tried to rescue, a freezing and befuddled soldier who thought he was a wolf and ran him through with his sword. But another account says Barry retired and lived out his old age in comfort. Either way, his body was stuffed when he died and is still on display in the Berne Natural History Museum in Switzerland.

Dogs are big enough to be companions but not so big as to overwhelm us.

The dog's furry coat is another reason we favor them. People have a strong preference for furry animals. Fur is pleasing to the touch. Perhaps that's one reason why pigs, which are very intelligent and can be very affectionate, have never become truly popular pets. They are bristly, not pleasant to the touch.

During a training session, a specially trained search dog inspects a pile of rubble.

SOCIAL BEHAVIOR

Dogs are social animals, and that is probably the most important reason they have become so close to people. This is one way in which dogs differ from cats. A cat is a solitary, independent animal, but a dog wants to fit in, wants to conform to the ways of the human pack. This goes back to its wild heritage. Lone wolves cannot kill large animals. Hunting requires the cooperation of the whole pack, so each wolf is loyal and protective of the pack as a group. The dog transfers these feelings to the human family, protecting it and its home from intruders.

In the wild, wolves are able to make plans before starting a hunt. They use encircling and ambushing techniques to trap their prey. Those same qualities have been put to use by people in training dogs to herd other domesticated animals, such as sheep and cattle, and in hunting to track and flush out game. Dogs are also able to keep their aggressive tendencies in check. Within the wolf pack, individual members establish a **hierarchy**, so that it is clear which animals are the leaders and which are the followers. If there is a dispute, it is usually settled without an all-out fight because such fights would injure or kill individual members, and weaken the pack. In the same way, dogs respect the leadership of their human masters. They will rarely bite or attack them and will even allow themselves to be punished without striking back.

We also like dogs because they are good communicators. Within the life of the pack, wolves continually communicate with each other through body language. They use various postures to demonstrate dominance and submission and use signals to coordinate activities on the hunt. Because of this ability, they are very good at reading human moods and intentions and can show us a wide range of emotions. Their ability to be affectionate, to present themselves for petting, to lick our faces, and to cuddle up are all qualities that makes us feel very close to dogs.

Another important behavior is the dog's playfulness. Wolves are naturally playful. In the wild, they have been observed picking up sticks and inviting another to chase

A Dalmatian romps in the surf. Like their wolf ancestors, dogs are playful.

A Border collie helps a shepherd guide a flock of sheep through a maze of gates and pens. Some dogs work alongside humans.

them. These playful qualities have been accentuated in the dog, which, like all domesticated animals, retains more juvenile qualities into adulthood.

THE RIGHT PLACE, THE RIGHT TIME

But even with all these natural tendencies, dogs would not have become our most favored companions had wolves and primitive people not found themselves living so close together. Primates, such as chimpanzees and gorillas, are

A guide dog helps a blind woman negotiate a sidewalk.

How Long Do Dogs Live?

Most dogs live between 8 and 15 years. The longest recorded life span for a dog is 29 years and 5 months. The dog, an Australian cattle dog named Bluey, died in 1939.

more reclusive. They don't make their homes on the fringes of the human community in order to scavenge food, as wolves did. Frequent opportunities for people to capture and raise young wolves are what began the whole process of wolves becoming dogs.

Dogs are the way they are because they are human-made animals. Many of the qualities they have are there because people—first unintentionally, then intentionally—bred these qualities into them. Today, loyalty to people is what makes the dog different from all other pets. Dogs have been known to travel hundreds, even thousands, of miles to be reunited with their owners. They will rescue people from burning homes, protect their owners from intruders, keep vigils waiting for owners to return even after the owners have died. Dogs have been trained to guide blind people and to rescue lost travelers. No wonder they are called "man's best friend."

archaeology The study of the way humans or animals lived a very long time ago. Archaeologists dig up the remains of ancient cities or settlements and study the bones, weapons, pottery, and other things they find. They also dig up the remains of animals and study their bones to understand how they lived and changed over time.

breed A group of animals that have been changed by man. A breed is created by picking specific animals to mate and have offspring. As a result these animals have a particular uniform appearance, as in the case of such dogs as the dachshund, the poodle, or the bulldog.

canid Refers to the group, *Canis*, to which dogs and wolves belong.

Canis The Latin word for dog. It is the name biologists give to the group, or genus, to which dogs and wolves belong.

domestication The act of training or changing a wild animal to bring out traits considered useful.

feral A wild animal, particularly one that was formerly tame or **domesticated**.

genes The tiny units of a cell of an animal or plant that determine the characteristics that an offspring inherits from its parent or parents.

genus A classification of plants or animals with common characteristics.

hierarchy The order of leadership within a pack or herd of animals. Within a wolf pack, for example, one wolf will often be recognized as the leader. Below that wolf each wolf has a sense of where it fits into the chain of command, with the weakest or youngest wolves being lowest in importance.

hygiene Things that must be done to keep people or animals and places healthy and clean.

marked stop The sharp angle on the skull of an animal where the forehead meets the muzzle.

selective breeding The mating of animals with specific traits to produce offspring with a particular uniform appearance or behavior.

FOR FURTHER INFORMATION

BOOKS

Emert, Phyllis. *Search-and-Rescue Dogs*. New York: Crestwood House, 1994.

Hughes, Dean. *Dog Detectives and Other Amazing Canines*. New York: Random House, 1994.

Kappeler, Markus. *Dogs Wild & Domestic*. Milwaukee, WI: Gareth Stevens, 1991.

Piers, Helen. *Taking Care of Your Dog*. Hauppauge, NY: Barron's, 1992.

Pinkwater, Jill, and Daniel Pinkwater. *Superpuppy: How to Choose, Raise, and Train the Best Possible Dog for You*. New York: Clarion, 1979.

Roalf, Peggy. *Dogs*. New York: Hyperion, 1993.

Silverstein, Alvin, and Virginia Silverstein. *Dogs: All About Them*. New York: Lathrop, 1986.

Squire, Ann. *Understanding Man's Best Friend: Why Dogs Look and Act the Way They Do*. New York: Macmillan, 1991.

———. *101 Questions and Answers about Pets and People*. New York: Macmillan, 1988.

For Advanced Readers

Caras, Roger A. *A Dog Is Listening*. New York: Simon & Schuster, 1992.

Clutton-Brock, Juliet. *A Natural History of Domesticated Animals*. Austin: University of Texas Press, 1989.

Fogle, Bruce. *The Dog's Mind*. New York: Macmillan, 1990.

Haddon, Celia. *Faithful to the End*. New York: St. Martin's Press, 1991.

Hearne, Vicki. *Adam's Task: Calling Animals by Name*. New York: Knopf, 1986.

Lorenz, Konrad. *Man Meets Dog*. New York: Houghton Mifflin, 1955.

Morris, Desmond. *Dogwatching*. New York: Crown, 1986.

Serpel, James. *In the Company of Animals*. New York: Cambridge University Press, 1996.

Thomas, Elizabeth Marshall. *The Hidden Life of Dogs*. New York: Houghton Mifflin, 1993.

Winokur, Jon. *Mondo Canine*. New York: Penguin, 1991.

INTERNET SITES

Because of the changeable nature of the Internet, sites appear and disappear very quickly. These resources offered useful information on dogs at the time of publication. Internet addresses must be entered with capital and lowercase letters exactly as they appear.

http://www.yahoo.com
The Yahoo directory of the World Wide Web is an excellent place to find Internet sites on any topic.

http://www.akc.org/
This is the home page of the American Kennel Club.

http://www.aspca.org/
This is the home page of the American Society for the Prevention of Cruelty to Animals (ASCPA), an organization dedicated to promoting humane treatment of animals.

http://www.woofs
This site is dedicated to the adoption and care of dogs.

http://www.thepetchannel.com
This site provides resources for pet owners.

http://www.iup.edu/~wolf/wolves.htmlx
This site provides lots of information on wolves, including resources, pictures, and links.

INDEX

Page numbers in *italics* indicate illustrations.

Africa, 9
Airedale terriers, 27
Akitas, 27
Alaska, 11
Alpha wolves, 12
American foxhounds, 39
American Kennel Club
 (AKC), 39
Anatomy, 18, *18*, 27
Arabian desert wolf, 16
Archaeology, 17–22, *19*, *20*

Arctic fox, 11
Asia, 9, 32, 42
Asian wolf, 16, *17*
Assyrians, 32
Australia, 42
Australian cattle dogs, 53

Barking, 28, 34
Barry, 48
Basset hounds, 36
Beagles, *33*

Belgian Sheepdogs, *21*
Berne Natural History
    Museum (Switzerland), 48
Beta wolves, 12
Bloodhounds, 28, 36
Border collies, *52*
Breeding, 9, 11, 13, 15,
    23–29, 30, 33, 35–38
    selective, 25–9
Brooke, Robert, 39
Bulldogs, 27, 38, *39*

Canada, 11
Canis lupus pallipes, 16, *17*
Chihuahuas, *24*, 30
Chinese, 35, 41
Cocker spaniels, 27
Columella, 33
Coyotes, 24, 28

Dalmatians, 31, 36, 51
Dingoes, *41*, 42
Dog shows, 40
Domestication, 9, 17, 20, 22,
    23–29, 50, 52

Ears, 27
Easton Down, England, 22
Egyptians, ancient, 31
England, 22
Europe, 9
European wolves, 20

Feral dogs, 41
Fur, 11, 27, 48

Genes, 25
Golden retrievers, 27, 36–38
Gray wolves, 13

Great Danes, *24*, 30
Greenland, 11
Greyhounds, 22, 27, 31–32,
    36
Grime's Grave, England, 22
Guide dogs, 53, 54
*Guinness Book of Pet
    Records*, 25

Hearing, 36
Hierarchy, 50
Howling, 11
Hunting, 11, 12, *13*, 19, 31,
    36–38, 50
Huskies, 27
Hygiene, 44–46

Ice Age, 11
Indian dogs, 42
Indian wolf, 16
Inuit people, 11, *14*
Israel, 15

Jackals, 21
Jack Russell terriers, *27*
Jaguar Cave, Idaho, 22
Jarmo, Iraq, 20

Ken-L-Ration dog food, 48
Kublai Khan, 38

Labrador retrievers, 36–38,
    38
Life spans, 53

Marked stops, 22
Mastiffs, 31, 32, *32*, 33, 38
Mexico, 30
Miniature breeds, 25, 28

Museum of Natural History (Mexico City), 30

New Guinea, 42
North America, 9

Palegawra, Iraq, 20
Panting, 20
Pariah dogs, 42
Pekingese, 35–36, *35*
Pembroke Welsh corgis, 27
Piy dogs, 42
Pliny, 33
Pomeranian sheepdogs, 27
Poodles, 31, 36–38

St. Bernards, 30, 31, 48
Selective breeding. *See* Breeding
Shar-pei, 41
Sheepdogs, 27, *34*, 35
Shyness, 9
Siberia, 11
Singing dogs, 42

Sixth sense, the, 47
Skye terriers, 27
Sled dogs, 14
Smell, 45
Smiling, 28–29
Sociability, 11–13, 49–52
Spaniels, 45

Tails, 26, 27
Terriers, 25, *26*, 27, 36
Toy breeds. *See* Miniature breeds

United States, 22, 38

Vision, 24
Vlasac, Romania, 22

Whippets, 27
Windmill Hill, England, 22
Wolf-dog hybrids, 37, *37*
Wolf packs, *10*, 11, 12, 49–50

Yorkshire terrier, 25, 27

ABOUT THE AUTHOR

JOHN ZEAMAN is a journalist. For the past thirteen years, he has been a critic, feature writer, and editor with the *Bergen Record* of New Jersey. His interest in pets and animal domestication stems from the numerous pets that have lived in his household, including a standard poodle, two cats, gerbils, a parakeet, finches, lizards, turtles, a garter snake, and, briefly, a wild squirrel. The idea for this series grew out of a project that his daughter did in the fifth grade on the origins of pets. He lives in Leonia, New Jersey, with his wife, Janet, and their children, Claire and Alex.